Discovering Dinosaurs

SMALL AND DEADLY DINOSAURS

Consulting Editor: Carl Mehling

Skyview
Books

an imprint of
WINDMILL BOOKS
New York

Published in 2010 by Windmill Books, LLC
303 Park Avenue South, Suite # 1280, New York, NY 10010-3657

CREDITS:
Consulting Editor: Carl Mehling
Designer: Graham Beehag

567.9
Mehling

Publisher Cataloging in Publication

Small and deadly dinosaurs / consulting editor, Carl Mehling.
p. cm. – (Discovering dinosaurs)
Summary: With the help of fossil evidence this book provides physical descriptions of twenty-four small dinosaurs with predatory habits.—Contents: Eoraptor—Coelophysis—Herrerasaurus—Protoavis—Staurikosaurus—Gasosaurus—Proceratosaurus—Coelurus—Ornitholestes—Compsognathus—Becklespinax—Deinonychus—Pelicanimimus—Adasaurus—Alvarezsaurus—Anserimimus—Borogovia—Dromaeosaurus—Elmisaurus—Noasaurus—Oviraptor—Troodon—Velociraptor—Mononykus.
ISBN 978-1-60754-776-1. – ISBN 978-1-60754-784-6 (pbk.)
ISBN 978-1-60754-858-4 (6-pack)
1.   Dinosaurs—Juvenile literature   2. Carnivora, Fossil—Juvenile literature
[1. Dinosaurs   2. Predatory animals]   I. Mehling, Carl   II. Series
567.9/12—dc22

Printed in the United States

CPSIA Compliance Information: Batch #BW10W: For further information contact Windmill Books, New York, New York at 1-866-478-0556.

CONTENTS

Introduction

Imagining what our world was like in the distant past is a lot like being a detective. There were no cameras around, and there were no humans writing history books. In many cases, fossils are all that remain of animals who have been extinct for millions of years.

Fossils are the starting point that scientists use to make educated guesses about what life was like in prehistoric times. And while fossils are important, even the best fossil can't tell the whole story. If snakes were extinct, and all we had left were their bones, would anyone guess that they could snatch bats from the air in pitch-black caves? Probably not, but there is a Cuban species of snake that can do just that. Looking at a human skeleton wouldn't tell you how many friends that person had, or what their favorite color was. Likewise, fossils can give us an idea of how an animal moved and what kind of food it ate, but they can't tell us everything about an animal's behavior or what life was like for them.

Our knowledge of prehistoric life is constantly changing to fit the new evidence we have. While we may never know everything, the important thing is that we continue to learn and discover. Learning about the history of life on Earth, and trying to piece together the puzzle of the dinosaurs, can help us understand more about our past and future.

Eoraptor

• **ORDER** • Saurischia • **FAMILY** [unranked] • **GENUS & SPECIES** • *Eoraptor lunensis*

VITAL STATISTICS

FOSSIL LOCATION	Argentina
DIET	Carnivorous, possibly also a scavenger
PRONUNCIATION	EE-oh-RAP-tor
WEIGHT	22 lb (10 kg)
LENGTH	3 ft (1 m)
HEIGHT	20 in (50 cm)
MEANING OF NAME	"Dawn thief" because it was an early carnivorous dinosaur

Only identified in 1993, *Eoraptor* was one of the earliest dinosaurs, a meat-eating beast that stood up on two long hind legs and tore its prey apart with its large claws.

MOUTH
Eoraptor's mouth had dozens of teeth that were clearly designed for a carnivorous diet.

WHERE IN THE WORLD?

It was discovered in 1991 in the Ischigualasto Badlands in northwestern Argentina. This area was a river valley at the time *Eoraptor* existed but is now desert.

FOSSIL EVIDENCE

This is one of the few early dinosaurs for which an entire skeleton has been found. With its light, hollow bones and long, thin legs ending in three-toed feet, *Eoraptor* was built for speed. It stayed stable by keeping its tail out behind it. It simply outran its victims and then ripped them apart with its claws or teeth. *Eoraptor* was able to stay upright on two legs because of the strength provided by fused vertebrae in its hip region.

HOW BIG IS IT?

DINOSAUR

TRIASSIC

Hands
Eoraptor had five digits at the end of each "hand," three of them forming long claws. The other two digits were shorter.

TIMELINE (millions of years ago)

540	505	438	408	360	280	248	208	146	65	1.8 to today

Coelophysis

VITAL STATISTICS

Fossil Location	United States
Diet	Carnivorous
Pronunciation	SEE-low-FIE-sis
Weight	100 lb (45 kg)
Length	8–10 ft (2.5–3 m)
Height	Unknown
Meaning of name	"Hollow form" in reference to its light, hollow bones

One of the earliest dinosaurs, *Coelophysis* was a carnivore. It may have been a scavenger, but it was an efficient predator too. With powerful hind legs and a long, slender body, it was built to be fast. Almost hollow leg bones, and a skull with large fenestrae (openings), reduced its body weight, further increasing its speed. Its long, flexible neck, with a pronounced curve, helped it to grab its prey. *Coelophysis* may also have hunted in packs, which would have enabled it to take on large prey.

WHERE IN THE WORLD?

Certainly found in Arizona and New Mexico, *Coelophysis* may have ranged across the vast landmass.

FOSSIL EVIDENCE

Many specimens of *Coelophysis* have been discovered at the Ghost Ranch, New Mexico. This is a site rich in fossils. It includes a "graveyard" filled with hundreds of specimens—possibly victims of a flash flood. Scientists have found two different kinds of remains, which they think represent male ("robust") and female ("gracile") adult Coelophysis. It was once thought that *Coelophysis* ate its young—the stomachs of many adult specimens seemed to contain young *Coelophysis*, but later studies showed that these were other reptiles, not young Coelophysis.

HANDS
Strong three-fingered hands were used to clasp its prey.

JAW
Coelophysis had more than 100 daggerlike teeth, for ripping into flesh. A double hinge let it move its jaw back and forth, sawing its food.

DINOSAUR	
TRIASSIC	

HOW BIG IS IT?

• **ORDER** • Saurischia • **FAMILY** • Coelophysidae • **GENUS & SPECIES** • *Coelophysis bauri*

THE PETRIFIED FOREST

Coelophysis lived at a time when the world's landmass formed one supercontinent, known as Pangaea. It stayed mostly in the lowland environment, where the weather went from one extreme to another. Sometimes it was very hot and sometimes it was very cold. Flash floods were a problem, too. Flooding be the cause of the mass of skeletons found in the "graveyard" at the Ghost Ranch. Flooding probably created the Petrified Forest a crowded area of fossilized trees found in nearby Arizona.

TAIL
Its long, thin tail helped *Coelophysis* to hold its body almost horizontal to the ground while it ran.

HANDS
Hands equipped with three claws may have helped *Coelophysis* to dig prey from its burrow. A fourth claw that was useless was buried in its flesh.

TIMELINE (millions of years ago)

540	505	438	408	360	280	248	208	146	65	1.8 to today

Coelophysis

• **ORDER** • Saurischia • **FAMILY** • Coelophysidae • **GENUS & SPECIES** • *Coelophysis bauri*

CHANGING EARTH

Earth looked very different in the Late Triassic period when *Coelophysis* roamed the planet. North America, where lots of *Coelophysis* remains were found, was still part of Pangaea, one giant supercontinent. Sea levels in the Late Triassic were generally low and the climate in which *Coelophysis* lived could be extremely dry and hot. Much of *Coelophysis*'s home territory was desert. The look of the land was changing, too. Forests were starting to grow. Ferns and two types of seed plants, the cycads and the bennettitales, were growing everywhere on the forest floors. In North America, animals who shared this environment with *Coelophysis* included *Massospondylus*, one of the first known prosauropods and *Protosuchus*, one of the earliest crocodiles (both from Arizona). Then, suddenly, a mass extinction 200 million years ago wiped out more than half of all animal species then living on Earth and dinosaurs like *Coelophysis* and their descendants became the main land vertebrates on the planet.

Herrerasaurus

VITAL STATISTICS

FOSSIL LOCATION	Argentina
DIET	Carnivorous
PRONUNCIATION	huh-RARE-ah-SAWR-us
WEIGHT	440–780 lb (200–350 kg)
LENGTH	10 ft (3 m)
HEIGHT	Unknown
MEANING OF NAME	"Herrera's lizard" after Victorino Herrera, a rancher who discovered the fossil

FOSSIL EVIDENCE

The best specimens of *Herrerasaurus* were discovered by chance. Luckily, two almost complete skeletons were found. The specimens were so well preserved that tiny earbones were visible, as well as plates in the iris of the eyes. With the discovery of these findings, *Herrerasaurus* could be reconstructed for the first time. Partly healed toothmarks found on the skulls suggests that it lived in packs, fighting to win its place.

DINOSAUR

TRIASSIC

One of the earliest carnivorous dinosaurs, *Herrerasaurus* lived in South America, at a time when dinosaurs were just starting to appear. Its large serrated teeth could cut bone. Its powerful back legs and long stiff tail probably made it a fast runner. But this predator still had enemies: for example, scientists found a *Herrerasaurus* skill with puncture wounds in it. They looked like the bite marks of *Saurosuchus*, a giant reptile from the same time.

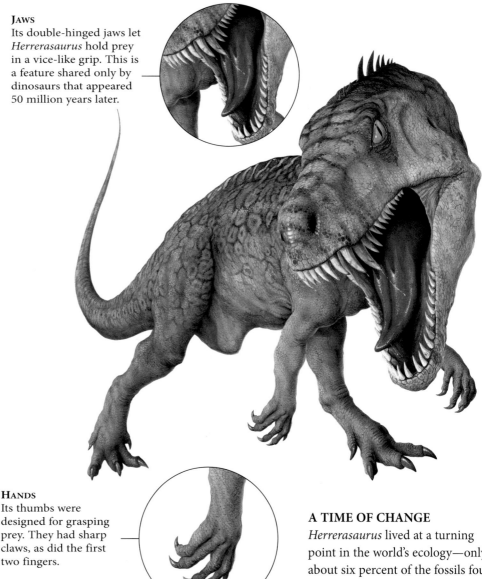

JAWS
Its double-hinged jaws let *Herrerasaurus* hold prey in a vice-like grip. This is a feature shared only by dinosaurs that appeared 50 million years later.

HANDS
Its thumbs were designed for grasping prey. They had sharp claws, as did the first two fingers.

HOW BIG IS IT?

A TIME OF CHANGE

Herrerasaurus lived at a turning point in the world's ecology—only about six percent of the fossils found from that time are from dinosaurs. By the end of the Triassic Period, though, dinosaurs were beginning to dominate on land. In fact, it was mostly dinosaurs that survived the end of that period. That meant surviving a mass extinction and volcanic eruptions which broke up the world's landmass.

• **ORDER** • Saurischia • **FAMILY** • Herrerasauridae • **GENUS & SPECIES** • *Herrerasaurus ischigualastensis*

WHERE IN THE WORLD?

To date, *Herrerasaurus* has been located only in northwest Patagonia, Argentina.

CONFUSED EVOLUTION

It is difficult to draw up a family tree for *Herrerasaurus*. It shares features with dinosaurs from the much later Jurassic Period; Unlike other dinosaurs living at the same time, Herrerasaurus had cone-shaped teeth and short arms for grabbing prey. Growing to lengths of up to 10 ft (3 m) it reached a size not seen again until the dinosaurs of the Jurassic.

BODY
The color of any dinosaur is a matter of guesswork, but *Herrerasaurus* may have had camouflage markings for hiding in undergrowth.

TIMELINE (millions of years ago)

| 640 | 505 | 438 | 408 | 360 | 280 | 248 | 208 | 146 | 65 | 1.8 to today |

Herrerasaurus

• **ORDER** • Saurischia • **FAMILY** • Herrerasauridae • **GENUS & SPECIES** • *Herrerasaurus ischigualastensis*

HERRERASAURUS DISCOVERY

Herrerasaurus was discovered in the Ischigualasto Formation of northwest Argentina in 1958. This first find was only part of a skeleton, but a complete skeleton, skull, and some more parts were found in 1988. This second find let scientists reconstruct a whole *Herrerasaurus* and learn a lot about its dinosaur characteristics. Scientists found that its pelvis was like a carnivorous dinosaur. But *Herrerasaurus*'s hipbones and legbones were more like an archosaur. At one time, archosaurs were the most common species on Earth. But, after about 50 million years, a climate change caused a mass extinction. Only a few archosaurs survived and their dinosaur descendants moved to the top.

Protoavis

• **ORDER** • Saurischia (disputed) • **FAMILY** • Protoavidae • **GENUS & SPECIES** • *Protoavis texensi*

VITAL STATISTICS

FOSSIL LOCATION	United States
DIET	Carnivorous
PRONUNCIATION	PRO-toe-A-vis
WEIGHT	12 oz (350 g)
LENGTH	14 in (35 cm)
HEIGHT	Unknown
MEANING OF NAME	"Early bird" because it was thought to be a bird

WHERE IN THE WORLD?

Found in a mixed-up group of crushed dinosaur bones in a Texan quarry.

Is it a bird? Is it a theropod dinosaur? This is one of the most hotly disputed creatures among paleontologists. If it really was avian (related to birds), it means birds first appeared several million decades earlier than previously thought.

FOSSIL EVIDENCE

The bones thought to belong to *Protoavis* were found in a pile of various dinosaur fossils. They include a section of the skull (a partly toothless jaw) and some limb bones. When put together, the bones suggest a creature with a bird-like skeleton with a tail, dinosaur-like back legs, and hollow bones. This has caused a lot of debate among paleontologists. Most paleontologists think the bones found came from different creatures, not one creature who looked like this. However, most paleontologists dispute whether the bones are from the same creature at all. If it was a primitive bird, *Protoavis* would have lived 75 million years before the famous *Archaeopteryx*, which would mean that the first birds lived among the first dinosaurs.

DINOSAUR
TRIASSIC

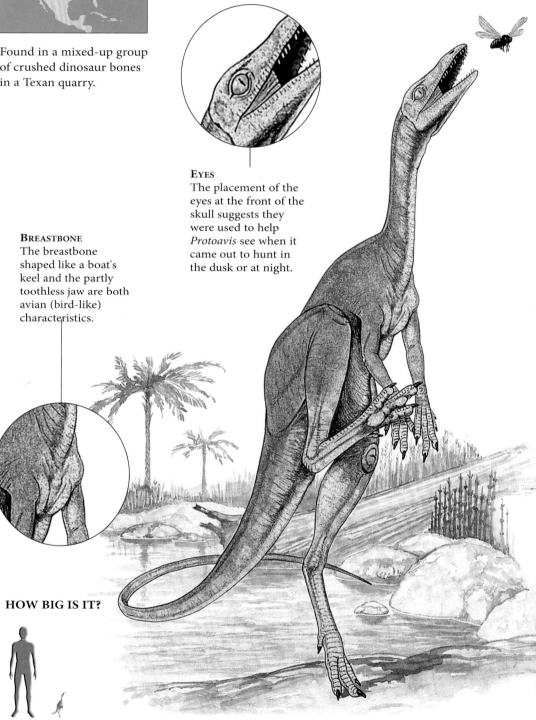

EYES
The placement of the eyes at the front of the skull suggests they were used to help *Protoavis* see when it came out to hunt in the dusk or at night.

BREASTBONE
The breastbone shaped like a boat's keel and the partly toothless jaw are both avian (bird-like) characteristics.

HOW BIG IS IT?

TIMELINE (millions of years ago)

540	505	438	408	360	280	248	208	146	65	1.8 to today

Staurikosaurus

• ORDER • Saurischia • FAMILY • Staurikosauridae • GENUS & SPECIES • *Staurikosaurus pricei*

VITAL STATISTICS

FOSSIL LOCATION	South America
DIET	Carnivorous
PRONUNCIATION	STAW-rick-oh-SAWR-US
WEIGHT	62 lb (28 kg)
LENGTH	7 ft (2 m)
HEIGHT	32 in (80 cm)
MEANING OF NAME	"Southern Cross lizard," after a constellation seen only in the Southern Hemisphere

FOSSIL EVIDENCE

There aren't many remains, because fossils rarely form in the forest environment where *Staurikosaurus* lived. However, because this was an early, primitive theropod, paleontologists think they can picture the entire animal. It was small, with a large head on a slender neck. Long, muscular legs ended on five-toed feet, while the shorter forearms had four-digit hands. It balanced using its long, thin tail. A sliding joint in the lower jaw allowed it to flex back and forth to work prey back toward the throat, a feature that later theropods no longer had.

DINOSAUR

LATE TRIASSIC

This was one of the earliest dinosaurs, a speedy, carnivorous beast.

TEETH
The sharp, backward-curving teeth set in a large head are thought by some to be big enough to allow *Staurikosaurus* to attack animals larger than itself.

LEGS
Large hind legs probably made this animal the fastest on land for its time—a huge advantage for a meat eater.

HOW BIG IS IT?

WHERE IN THE WORLD?

The few remains were found in Brazil and Argentina.

TIMELINE (millions of years ago)

| 540 | 505 | 438 | 408 | 360 | 280 | 248 | 208 | 146 | 65 | 1.8 to today |

Gasosaurus

• **ORDER** • Saurischia • **FAMILY** • Avetheropoda • **GENUS & SPECIES** • *Gasosaurus constructu*

VITAL STATISTICS

FOSSIL LOCATION	China
DIET	Carnivorous
PRONUNCIATION	GAS-oh-SAWR-us
WEIGHT	331 lb (150 kg)
LENGTH	11 ft (3.5 m)
HEIGHT	4 ft (1.3 m)
MEANING OF NAME	"Gas lizard" after the gas-mining company that discovered the fossil

FOSSIL EVIDENCE

Only one specimen of *Gasosaurus* has been discovered. The incomplete skeleton means that some of *Gasosaurus*'s features are based on guesswork and some scientists think that it is the same species as *Kaijiangosaurus*. *Gasosaurus* was a bipedal dinosaur with short arms that each ended in three sharp claws, which it used to seize and rip the flesh of its victims. *Gasosaurus* possessed the typical theropod tail that was held out stiffly for balance as it ran. Its hollow bones lightened its frame and made it a speedy predator.

The *Gasosaurus* fossil narrowly escaped being destroyed by bulldozers. Fragments of the dinosaur's bones were discovered when a Chinese natural gas company was clearing land to build a field facility.

TEETH
The knifelike teeth were used to puncture, slice, and restrain prey. Theropods such as *Gasosaurus* might have dealt deadly bites to victims' heads.

WHERE IN THE WORLD?

China's Shaximiao Formation is practically a dinosaur quarry. More than 8,000 bones have been recovered from the site.

HOW BIG IS IT?

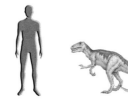

FEET
Its three toes spread as *Gasosaurus* walked on hard ground and closed when it lifted its foot, similar to the step of modern birds.

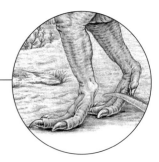

DINOSAUR

MID–JURASSIC

TIMELINE (millions of years ago)

540	505	438	408	360	280	248	208	146	65	1.8 to today

Proceratosaurus

• **ORDER** • Saurischia • **FAMILY** • Coelurosauria • **GENUS & SPECIES** • *Proceratosaurus bradleyi*

VITAL STATISTICS

Fossil Location	England
Diet	Carnivorous
Pronunciation	Pro-ser-RAT-uh-SAWR-us
Weight	220 lb (100 kg)
Length	Up to 10 ft (3 m)
Height	Unknown
Meaning of name	"Before *Ceratosaurus*" because of the belief it was Ceratosaurus's ancestor

Proceratosaurus was originally identified as an ancestor of *Ceratosaurus* because both had small crests on their snouts. Now scientists have decided that *Proceratosaurus* is an early coelurosaur.

WHERE IN THE WORLD?

Discovered in Gloucestershire, England, the fossil of Proceratosaurus is kept in London's Natural History Museum.

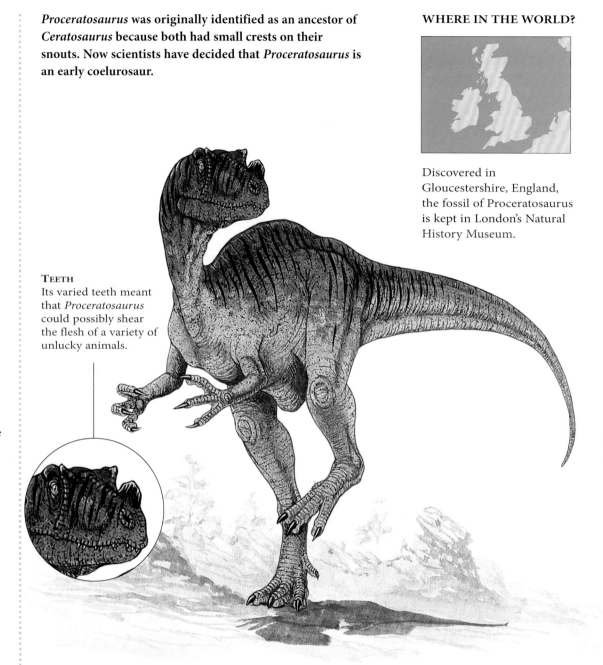

TEETH
Its varied teeth meant that *Proceratosaurus* could possibly shear the flesh of a variety of unlucky animals.

FOSSIL EVIDENCE

Scientists have only found part of a skull of *Proceratosaurus*. From this fossil, scientists learned that this creature had a small, bony crest on top of its snout. This reminded paleontologists of *Ceratosaurus*'s crest. Its function is still a mystery. Some believe the dinosaur's crest attracted females of the species. The jaw of *Proceratosaurus* was lined with smaller, more cone-shaped teeth in front than in the back. Having more than one type of tooth allowed *Proceratosaurus* to eat a wider variety of foods.

HOW BIG IS IT?

LOWER LEG
Typical of coelurosaurs, the lower leg bone is longer than the upper leg bone, making *Proceratosaurus* a good runner.

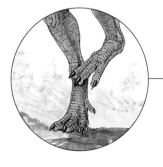

DINOSAUR

MID-JURASSIC

TIMELINE (millions of years ago)

| 40 | 505 | 438 | 408 | 360 | 280 | 248 | 208 | 146 | 65 | 1.8 to today |

Coelurus

• **ORDER** • Saurischia • **FAMILY** • Coeluridae • **GENUS & SPECIES** • *Coelurus fragil*

VITAL STATISTICS

FOSSIL LOCATION	Western US
DIET	Carnivorous
PRONUNCIATION	See-LURE-us
WEIGHT	44 lb (20 kg)
LENGTH	7 ft (2 m)
HEIGHT	6 ft (1.8 m)
MEANING OF NAME	"Hollow tail" because of its hollow tail bones

FOSSIL EVIDENCE

Coelurus had a long, light tail with hollow vertebrae. *Coelurus*'s tail helped it to balance and steer. It could make sharp turns and change direction while running at top speed. Its long, slender legs were powerful, making *Coelurus* a good runner that could easily jump on prey. This also made *Coelurus* good at avoiding large, hungry carnivores. With its small, sharp teeth, *Coelurus* probably ate lizards and small mammals that it may have leaped on and taken by surprise.

Coelurus was a bipedal carnivore with long legs and a light-weight skeleton that made it an athletic runner. Its speed helped it make kills and avoid larger predators.

HANDS
Coelurus's three-fingered hand ended in curved claws that tightly grasped and then punctured the struggling body of its victim.

WHERE IN THE WORLD?

The *Coelurus* fossil is stored at Yale University's Peabody Museum of Natural History in New Haven, Connecticut.

FOOT CLAWS
Coelurus may have stood on its prey and slashed open its belly with its claws, so it could get to its victim's tender internal organs.

HOW BIG IS IT?

DINOSAUR

LATE JURASSIC

TIMELINE (millions of years ago)

540	505	438	408	360	280	248	208	146	65	1.8 to today

Ornitholestes

ORDER • Saurischia • **FAMILY** • Coelurosauria • **GENUS & SPECIES** • *Ornitholestes hermanni*

VITAL STATISTICS

FOSSIL LOCATION	Western United States
DIET	Carnivorous
PRONUNCIATION	Or-NITH-oh-LESS-teez
WEIGHT	24 lb (11 kg)
LENGTH	7 ft (2 m)
HEIGHT	12 in (30 cm)
MEANING OF NAME	"Bird robber" because it was originally thought to eat birds

FOSSIL EVIDENCE

The light frame and strong, slim legs of *Ornitholestes* made it quick and flexible. Equipped with a balancing tail that helped in changing direction while running, *Ornitholestes* probably leaped at small mammals, lizards, or helpless baby dinosaurs. Its narrow head had jaws lined with sharp, cone-shaped teeth. The largest were located at the front of its mouth for biting and gripping its prey. A broken nasal bone in the fossil's skull led many scientists to believe incorrectly that *Ornitholestes* had a crest on its snout.

DINOSAUR

LATE JURASSIC

Ornitholestes was a fast, bipedal predator that sprinted after prey. As a small predator at a time when huge theropods ruled, *Ornitholestes* was always on guard, watching for danger with its large eyes.

TAIL
Its stiff tail helped with balance and steering, allowing it to make quick turns when charging after a victim.

THUMB
The third finger acted like a thumb, allowing *Ornitholestes* to get a death grip on its victims.

HOW BIG IS IT?

WHERE IN THE WORLD?

Wyoming was located in the western part of the super-continent Laurasia during the late Jurassic.

TIMELINE (millions of years ago)

40	505	438	408	360	280	248	208	146	65	1.8 to today

Compsognathus

ORDER • Saurischia • **FAMILY** • Compsognathidae • **GENUS & SPECIES** • *Compsognathus longip*

VITAL STATISTICS

FOSSIL LOCATION	Germany, France
DIET	Carnivorous
PRONUNCIATION	KOMP-sog-NAY-thus
WEIGHT	6.5 lb (3 kg)
LENGTH	2.3–4.6 ft (0.7–1.4 m)
HEIGHT	10 in (26 cm) at the hips
MEANING OF NAME	"Delicate jaw"

FOSSIL EVIDENCE

Compsognathus was a small, chicken-sized dinosaur. It ran after small prey on its long, thin legs. The bones of fast-running lizards discovered in its stomach proved that *Compsognathus* was swift. *Compsognathus*'s hands each had three claws that were perfect for gripping struggling victims. Its long tail acted as a counterbalance as the speedy dinosaur chased prey or made fast turns when fleeing predators. Recent fossil discoveries show that *Compsognathus* was probably covered in fine, downy feathers, which kept its body warm.

Compsognathus's fossil is so delicate and birdlike that it was used as an example in the argument that dinosaurs are the ancestors of modern-day birds.

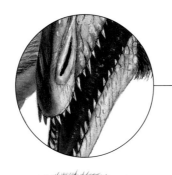

TEETH
Compsognathus had small, sharp teeth that were perfect for chomping down on lizards, insects, fish, and small mammals.

WHERE IN THE WORLD?

A *Compsognathus* fossil was discovered buried in limestone near Nice in southwestern France. It has also been found in Germany.

NECK
Using its long, flexible neck, *Compsognathus* could look around and watch for danger or scan the area for prey.

DINOSAUR
LATE JURASSIC

HOW BIG IS IT?

TIMELINE (millions of years ago)

540	505	438	408	360	280	248	208	146	65	1.8 to today

Becklespinax

• **ORDER** • Saurischia • **FAMILY** • Tetanurae • **GENUS & SPECIES** • *Becklespinax altispinax*

Becklespinax was a large theropod dinosaur that hunted the Cretaceous landscapes in search of prey. It is known from fossils with three vertebrae featuring tall spines that were discovered in England in 1884.

VITAL STATISTICS

FOSSIL LOCATION	England
DIET	Carnivorous
PRONUNCIATION	BECK-el-SPY-nax
WEIGHT	1,984 lb (900 kg)
LENGTH	16–26 ft (5–8 m)
HEIGHT	10 ft (3 m)
MEANING OF NAME	"Beckles' spine" in honor of Samuel Beckles who discovered the fossil

FOSSIL EVIDENCE

It was so difficult to figure out exactly what type of dinosaur *Becklespinax* was that it was not until 1991 that the theropod was assigned its current name. During the Cretaceous, *Becklespinax* probably stalked sauropods. It sank its knife-like claws into its victims, slicing open their hide so its sharp teeth could easily reach their muscles and internal organs. *Becklespinax's* strong jaws were able to tear away big hunks of meat that the dinosaur swallowed whole. When no live prey was available, *Becklespinax* may have scavenged for corpses.

DINOSAUR

EARLY CRETACEOUS

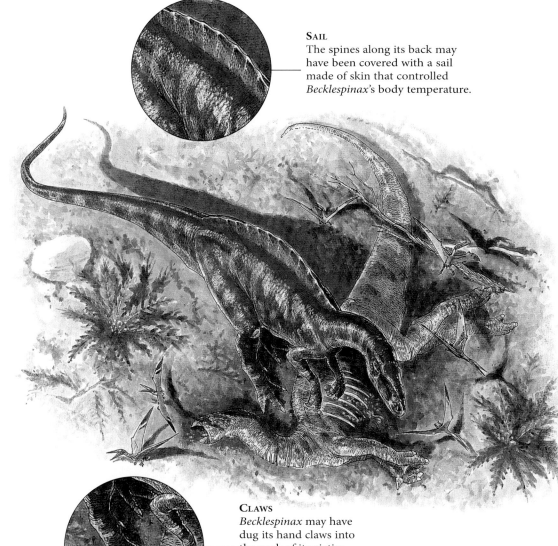

SAIL
The spines along its back may have been covered with a sail made of skin that controlled *Becklespinax's* body temperature.

CLAWS
Becklespinax may have dug its hand claws into the neck of its victim to steady itself while slashing away with its foot claws.

HOW BIG IS IT?

WHERE IN THE WORLD?

The fossil of *Becklespinax* was found in the sandstone of the Hastings Beds of East Sussex in England..

TIMELINE (millions of years ago)

40	505	438	408	360	280	248	208	146	65	1.8 to today

Deinonychus

VITAL STATISTICS

FOSSIL LOCATION	United States
DIET	Carnivorous
PRONUNCIATION	Die-NON-ih-kus
WEIGHT	160 lb (73 kg)
LENGTH	11 ft (3.4 m)
HEIGHT	4 ft (1.2 m)
MEANING OF NAME	"Terrible claw" after its sickle-like weapons

FOSSIL EVIDENCE

Deinonychus fossils were first uncovered in 1931, but the find did not receive much attention until 1969. In the meantime, more finds came to light. The discovery of several *Deinonychus* near a larger dinosaur suggests it may have hunted in packs, but scientists argue about this. After all, the herd may have been scavenging a corpse or the skeletons could have washed together in a river. Fossilized eggshells found very close to a skeleton have led to the suggestion that *Deinonychus* sat over its eggs, keeping them warm with body heat like modern birds do.

DINOSAUR

EARLY CRETACEOUS

Deinonychus was a small but deadly theropod. Its discovery made scientists take another look at the possible intelligence of dinosaurs. It also raised the question of whether dinosaurs were warm- or cold-blooded. Paleontologists disagree about whether it hunted in packs, how fast it could run, how it used its enlarged toe claw, and even the question of whether it is a birdlike dinosaur or a dinosaur-like bird. It is agreed that this was an intelligent predator with a large brain for its size and that it was a dangerous hunter.

WHERE IN THE WORLD?

Nine incomplete skeletons have been found in Montana, Oklahoma, Wyoming, Utah, and possibly Maryland.

HOW BIG IS IT?

• **ORDER** • Saurischia • **FAMILY** • Dromaeosauridae • **GENUS & SPECIES** • *Deinonychus antirrhopus*

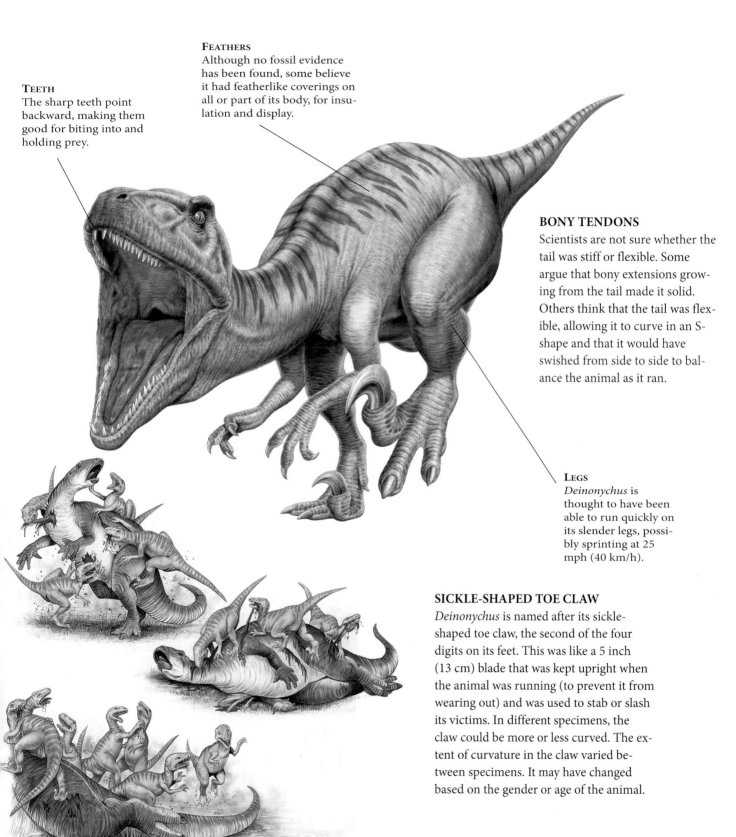

TEETH
The sharp teeth point backward, making them good for biting into and holding prey.

FEATHERS
Although no fossil evidence has been found, some believe it had featherlike coverings on all or part of its body, for insulation and display.

BONY TENDONS
Scientists are not sure whether the tail was stiff or flexible. Some argue that bony extensions growing from the tail made it solid. Others think that the tail was flexible, allowing it to curve in an S-shape and that it would have swished from side to side to balance the animal as it ran.

LEGS
Deinonychus is thought to have been able to run quickly on its slender legs, possibly sprinting at 25 mph (40 km/h).

SICKLE-SHAPED TOE CLAW
Deinonychus is named after its sickle-shaped toe claw, the second of the four digits on its feet. This was like a 5 inch (13 cm) blade that was kept upright when the animal was running (to prevent it from wearing out) and was used to stab or slash its victims. In different specimens, the claw could be more or less curved. The extent of curvature in the claw varied between specimens. It may have changed based on the gender or age of the animal.

TIMELINE (millions of years ago)

| 40 | 505 | 438 | 408 | 360 | 280 | 248 | 208 | 146 | 65 | 1.8 to today |

Deinonychus

• ORDER • Saurischia **• FAMILY •** Dromaeosauridae **• GENUS & SPECIES •** *Deinonychus antirrhopus*

HUNTING TACTICS

Some paleontologists believe that *Deinony-chus* not only hunted prey in gangs, but also used several deadly techniques when attacking dinosaurs much larger than themselves. Despite its small size, *Deinonychus* was a terrifyingly efficient killing machine, with all the equipment needed for destroying prey. Any victim who faced a whole gang of them probably stood little chance of survival. Some have suggested that this is what may have happened to the 27-foot (8 m)-long, 1.9-ton (2,000 kg) herbivore *Tenontosaurus*. Fossil remains make it look like this large herbivore was attacked by a group of *Deinonychus* more than a hundred million years ago, in an area that would now be part of the state of Montana. *Deinonychus'* toe claw was capable of ripping its victims open and tearing out their organs.

Pelicanimimus

• **ORDER** • Saurischia • **FAMILY** • Ornithomimosauridae • **GENUS & SPECIES** • *Pelicanimimus polyoda*

VITAL STATISTICS

FOSSIL LOCATION	Spain
DIET	Carnivorous
PRONUNCIATION	PEL-uh-kan-uh-MEEM-us
WEIGHT	Up to 55 lb (25 kg)
LENGTH	7 ft (2 m)
HEIGHT	Unknown
MEANING OF NAME	"Pelican mimic" in reference to its long face and the pouch beneath its jaw

FOSSIL EVIDENCE

Many well-preserved fossils have been found in La Hoyas, Spain, including *Pelicanimimus*. Impressions of its soft tissue in the limestone show a crest on the back of its head, and a featherless pouch beneath its jaw, like the modern pelican. It may have used this pouch for storing fish. Even muscle tissue was well preserved. Only one other fossil, from Brazil, has been this well preserved.

Walking upright on long hind legs, *Pelicanimimus* may have waded into water in search of prey. It caught its prey in the three long fingers of its hooklike hands.

TEETH
Pelicanimimus was one of very few ornithomimosaurs to have teeth; it had 220, which were small and peglike with sharp edges.

To date, *Pelicanimimus* has been found only in Spain.

SKIN
Fossil evidence suggests that *Pelicanimimus* may have had smooth, naked skin, without scales, feathers, or even hair.

HOW BIG IS IT?

DINOSAUR

EARLY CRETACEOUS

TIMELINE (millions of years ago)

540	505	438	408	360	280	248	208	146	65	1.8 to today

Adasaurus

• **ORDER** • Saurischia • **FAMILY** • Dromaeosauridae • **GENUS & SPECIES** • *Adasaurus mongoliensis*

VITAL STATISTICS

FOSSIL LOCATION	Mongolia
DIET	Carnivorous
PRONUNCIATION	ADD-ah-SAWR-us
WEIGHT	33 lb (15 kg)
LENGTH	7 ft (2 m)
HEIGHT	28 in (70 cm)
MEANING OF NAME	"Ada lizard" after a Mongolian mythological evil spirit

FOSSIL EVIDENCE

Two incomplete specimens have been found, but they gave paleontologists enough clues to figure out that this was a coelurosaur, a theropod closely related to birds. About the size of a large dog, it was intelligent, quick and agile, able to outsmart and outrun smaller prey. The second toe of each hind foot was a sickle-shaped claw that could be flicked like a switchblade to rip into its victims. This claw is larger in other dromaeosaurids, but the skull is higher than the *Velociraptor*, which *Adasaurus* closely resembles.

Named after a female Mongolian evil spirit that was able to take many forms, the arrival of *Adasaurus* spelled trouble for Late Cretaceous lizards and small mammals.

FEATHERS
As a dromaeosaurid, *Adasaurus* is likely to have been at least partially covered in feathers on its body and tail.

WHERE IN THE WORLD?

Both specimens are from Mongolia's Gobi Desert region.

HOW BIG IS IT?

DINOSAUR
LATE CRETACEOUS

CLAWS
The killer toe claw was held off the ground while *Adasaurus* moved to prevent it from getting damaged.

IMELINE (millions of years ago)

40	505	438	408	360	280	248	208	146	65	1.8 to today

Alvarezsaurus

• ORDER • Saurischia • FAMILY • Alvarezsauridae • GENUS & SPECIES • *Alvarezsaurus calvo*

VITAL STATISTICS

FOSSIL LOCATION	Argentina
DIET	Carnivorous
PRONUNCIATION	Al-vuh-rez-SAWR-us
WEIGHT	44 lb (20 kg)
LENGTH	7 ft (2 m)
HEIGHT	4.6 ft (1.4 m)
MEANING OF NAME	"Alvarez lizard" after the Argentine historian Gregorio Alvarez

WHERE IN THE WORLD?

Found in the Bajo de la Carpa Formation in Neuquén, Argentina.

This is one of the creatures that give paleontologists a headache. *Alvarezsaurus* has been classified at times as a non-avian theropod dinosaur and an early flightless bird. It may represent an important link between the two.

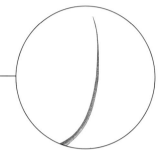

TAIL
Alvarezsaurus had an amazingly long tail, much like those seen in some modern lizards.

COMPACT BODY
There are practically no spines on the back vertebrae, so the body is compact with no ridges down its back, like a bird.

FOSSIL EVIDENCE

The weirdness of this animal and the lack of a complete skull or forelimbs among the remains explain the classification problem. *Alvarezsaurus* had very long, slender legs ending in long feet, short arms, and an extended, thin, flat tail that made up more than half of its length. The long, flexible S-shaped neck ended in a small skull with small unserrated teeth in the snout. It couldn't fly, but it was very fast and agile.

DINOSAUR

LATE CRETACEOUS

HOW BIG IS IT?

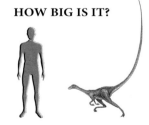

TIMELINE (millions of years ago)

540	505	438	408	360	280	248	208	146	65	1.8 to today

Anserimimus

• **ORDER** • Saurischia • **FAMILY** • Ornithomimidae • **GENUS & SPECIES** • *Anserimimus planinychus*

VITAL STATISTICS

Fossil Location	Mongolia
Diet	Carnivorous
Pronunciation	AN-ser-i-MIME-us
Weight	62 kg (137 lb)
Length	1 m (3 ft)
Height	Unknown
Meaning of name	"Goose mimic." "Anser" is the general name of several species of goose and ornithomimosaurs have traditionally been named after different types of birds

The ornithimids were so named because they mimic (or copy) ostriches by being long legged and flightless. In fact their skulls are more like those of New Zealand's extinct ground-dwelling birds. *Anserimimus* was a strong-armed species of the group.

WHERE IN THE WORLD?

The specimens were found in the Nemegt Formation of Mongolia.

FOSSIL EVIDENCE

Only parts of an incomplete forelimb and hind limb have been found of this species. These show several differences from other ornithimids. The hand claws are not curved, but long and straight, while the forelimb is more powerful, featuring attachments for large arm muscles. These suggest it dug for food, perhaps insects and dinosaur eggs and possibly even roots (since some paleontologists believe it added some plants to its mostly meat diet). The long shins and feet gave it speed, probably its only defense against attack.

BEAK
Anserimimus used its beak to pick food up and may have had a comblike structure to filter food particles in its mouth.

DINOSAUR

LATE CRETACEOUS

HOW BIG IS IT?

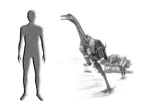

FINGERS
The fingers were positioned close together, almost like hoofs, and the claws were slightly flattened, features which scientists cannot fully explain.

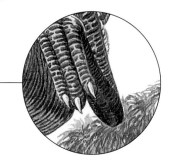

TIMELINE (millions of years ago)

540	505	438	408	360	280	248	208	146	65	1.8 to today

Borogovia

• **ORDER** • Saurischia • **FAMILY** • Troodontidae • **GENUS & SPECIES** • *Borogovia gracilicru*

VITAL STATISTICS

FOSSIL LOCATION	Mongolia
DIET	Carnivorous
PRONUNCIATION	Bor-oh-GOH-vee-a
WEIGHT	29 lb (13 kg)
LENGTH	7 ft (2 m)
HEIGHT	28 in (70 cm)
MEANING OF NAME	Named after the imaginary "borogoves" in Lewis Carroll's poem *Jabberwocky*

FOSSIL EVIDENCE

Only parts of a leg and a foot have been found, so most of what is known about *Borogovia* comes from studies of *Saurornithoides* and *Tochisaurus* similar animals whose remains were found at the same site. Some paleontologists suggest they are the same animal. *Borogovia* is a lightly built theropod with long, wiry legs, far slimmer than *Saurornithoides*. Each foot has a sicklelike killing claw. This claw is smaller and straighter than those found on other troodontids—they seem to have reduced in size as the group evolved.

"All mimsy were the borogoves," says Lewis Carroll's nonsense poem *Jabberwocky*, after which this animal was named. Very little is known about this dinosaur since very few remains have been found.

FEATHERED TAIL
This was a birdlike dinosaur and parts of its body and tail may have been feathered.

WHERE IN THE WORLD?

The remains were all found in Mongolia.

THIN TOES
The thin toes suggest that *Borogovia* had thin arms and legs so it was fast moving and, like other troodonts, quick thinking with its relatively large brain.

HOW BIG IS IT?

DINOSAUR

LATE CRETACEOUS

TIMELINE (millions of years ago)

540	505	438	408	360	280	248	208	146	65	1.8 to today

Dromaeosaurus

• **ORDER** • Saurischia • **FAMILY** • Dromaeosauridae
• **GENUS & SPECIES** • Several species within the genus *Dromaeosaurus*

VITAL STATISTICS

FOSSIL LOCATION	Canada, United States
DIET	Carnivorous
PRONUNCIATION	DROH-mee-oh-SAWR-us
WEIGHT	33 lb (15 kg)
LENGTH	6 ft (1.8 m)
HEIGHT	2 ft (0.7 m)
MEANING OF NAME	"Running lizard" because of its swiftness

FOSSIL EVIDENCE

Dromaeosaurus walked, ran, and leaped on powerful hind legs, killing prey with a sicklelike toe claw and a strong jaw equipped with backward-curving teeth. Its skull was larger than later dromaeosaurids and its teeth stronger— better for gripping than ripping. It may well have been partly feathered.

This was probably an intelligent, quick, and athletic wolf-sized predator with sharp senses and vicious teeth and claws. It may well have hunted in packs to take on much larger prey.

WHERE IN THE WORLD?

First found in the Judith River Formation of Canada, with some further remains in Montana.

STIFFENED TAIL
The tail was stiffened by a network of bony rods but was flexible enough to bend somewhat side to side.

HOW BIG IS IT?

TEETH
Remains of the serrated teeth show heavy wear, suggesting they wore down on the bones of its prey.

DINOSAUR

LATE CRETACEOUS

TIMELINE (millions of years ago)

| 40 | 505 | 438 | 408 | 360 | 280 | 248 | 208 | 146 | 65 | 1.8 to today |

Elmisaurus

• **ORDER** • Saurischia • **FAMILY** • Caenagnathidae • **GENUS & SPECIES** • *Elmisaurus rart*

VITAL STATISTICS

Fossil Location	Canada, Mongolia
Diet	Carnivorous
Pronunciation	ELM-ee-SAWR-us
Weight	71 lb (32 kg)
Length	7 ft (2 m)
Height	Unknown
Meaning of name	"Hind foot lizard" because of the peculiar fusing of the bones of its hind foot

FOSSIL EVIDENCE

Elmisaurus was discovered in Mongolia, and later finds in North America provide evidence that non-avian dinosaurs migrated. Its bones are so thin that they have not been well preserved in the fossil record, and only its hands, feet, and leg bones have been discovered. Elongated feet and shins suggest that it ran swiftly, while it probably used the three fingers on its clawed hands to grab insects and small animals. Similarities to the fossils of other dinosaurs enable paleontologists to make some guesses about its general appearance.

DINOSAUR

LATE CRETACEOUS

Elmisaurus walked on two legs and had hands with three digits on long arms. A member of the oviraptor group, it probably had a short, parrotlike skull and may have been feathered.

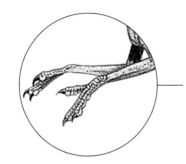

ARMS
Elmisaurus had arms that were longer and hands that were thinner than its relatives, the coelurosaurs.

WHERE IN THE WORLD?

To date, *Elmisaurus* has been located only in Mongolia and Canada.

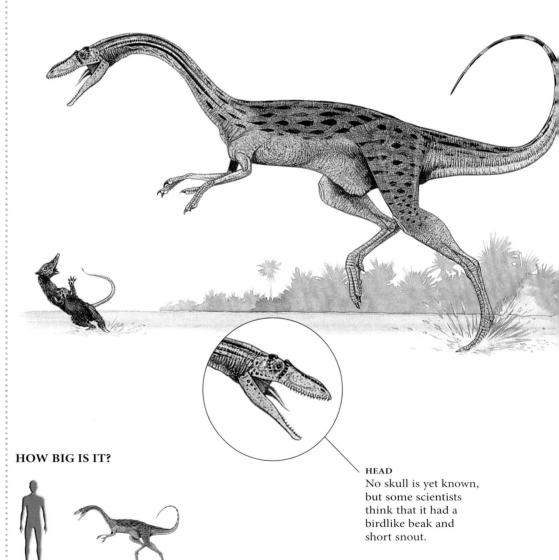

HEAD
No skull is yet known, but some scientists think that it had a birdlike beak and short snout.

HOW BIG IS IT?

TIMELINE (millions of years ago)

540	505	438	408	360	280	248	208	146	65	1.8 to today

Noasaurus

• **ORDER** • Saurischia • **FAMILY** • Abelisauridae • **GENUS & SPECIES** • *Noasaurus leali*

VITAL STATISTICS

FOSSIL LOCATION	Argentina
DIET	Carnivorous
PRONUNCIATION	NOH-ah-SAWR-us
WEIGHT	33 lb (15 kg)
LENGTH	6–8 ft (1.8–2.4 m)
HEIGHT	Unknown
MEANING OF NAME	"Northwestern Argentine lizard," in reference to where it was discovered ("NOA" abbreviates the Spanish *noroeste Argentina*)

FOSSIL EVIDENCE

Noasaurus shows how difficult the study of fossil evidence can be. It was first thought to have a retractable claw on the second toe of each foot, a feature found on *Dromaeosaurus*, a theropod not closely related. But, further study has led paleontologists to think that this claw actually belonged on its hand. At first, *Noasaurus* was assigned to the family of Noasauridae, but because of its lower jaw, similar to that of *Abelisaurus,* it has now been reassigned to the Abelisauridae.

DINOSAUR

LATE CRETACEOUS

Lightly built, *Noasaurus* was an efficient predator, and may have hunted in packs to attack young sauropods.

LEGS
Long legs made *Noasaurus* a swift runner. One of the fastest of its time, it was estimated to have reached speeds of 35 mph (56 km/h).

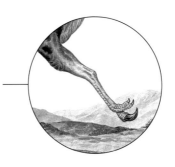

HAND CLAWS
Noasaurus had rather long arms, so it could make good use of its large claws to attack.

WHERE IN THE WORLD?

Noasaurus was located in what is now northwestern Argentina.

HOW BIG IS IT?

MELINE (millions of years ago)

40	505	438	408	360	280	248	208	146	65	1.8 to today

Oviraptor

VITAL STATISTICS

FOSSIL LOCATION	Mongolia, China
DIET	Possibly omnivorous
PRONUNCIATION	Ovi-RAP-tore
WEIGHT	44 lb (20 kg)
LENGTH	6 ft (19.6 m)
HEIGHT	2 ft 6 in (0.8 m)
MEANING OF NAME	"Egg thief" because the first specimen was found with eggs it was thought to be stealing

FOSSIL EVIDENCE

Although its skeleton was very bird-like and likely feathered, *Oviraptor* was a non-avian dinosaur. Its hands had three fingers with sharp claws more than 3 in (7 cm) long. It also had three-toed feet and a long, stiff tail. *Oviraptor*'s jaws were toothless and its diet is unknown, but since it was a theropod, it was likely at least partly carnivorous.

DINOSAUR

LATE CRETACEOUS

Oviraptor, which lived some 80 million years ago, had a crest on its head and a toothless beak. The crest was probably used for display in mating rituals. The first *Oviraptor* was discovered in the Gobi Desert of Mongolia in 1924, when a fossil was found on top of a clutch of eggs. At first, scientists thought the *Oviraptor* was stealing the eggs. Later, it appeared that the dinosaur was the egg layer, and was not necessarily an egg stealer after all.

BEAK
Oviraptor had a toothless beak. Further back in the mouth there was a pair of toothlike prongs.

Oviraptor was found in the Djadokhta Formation of Mongolia and the Neimongo Autonomous Region of Bayan Mandahu, China.

A CHANGING PICTURE
This illustration shows a featherless, egg-stealing *Oviraptor* (with a skull based on the crushed original find). Better fossils, including perfect skulls, changed scientists' ideas about the animal's appearance.

• **ORDER** • Saurischia • **FAMILY** • Oviraptoridae • **GENUS & SPECIES** • *Oviraptor philoceratops, O. mongoliensis*

HEAD CREST
There are many ideas about the crest on *Oviraptor*'s head, which was hollow and lined with a very thin sheet of bone. Although it may have had some unknown function, it's likely that *Oviraptor*'s crest was used mainly for species recognition.

STAR OF FILM AND TV
Today, *Oviraptor* has become a film and TV star, but its image has changed from egg thief to something more positive. In 2000, when the Walt Disney Pictures movie entitled *Dinosaur* was released, a computer-generated *Oviraptor* was shown stealing an *Iguanodon* egg. *Oviraptor* was later found to possibly be innocent of such types of theft. In 2002, it appeared in a TV miniseries based on James Gurney's *Dinotopia* in the more gentle character of Ovinutrix, which means "egg nurse."

BEAK
A mother *Oviraptor* may have used her beak to turn eggs to make sure that they would be warm.

EGG NURSE
Oviraptor adults protected their eggs by sitting over them as they lie in the nest.

HOW BIG IS IT?

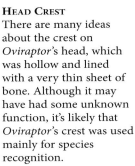

DEATH IN THE SAND
Sometimes sand covered, suffocated, and killed the brooding parent. Preserved by the sand for millions of years, the parent and its eggs were eventually found by paleontologists.

TIMELINE (millions of years ago)

540	505	438	408	360	280	248	208	146	65	1.8 to today

Oviraptor

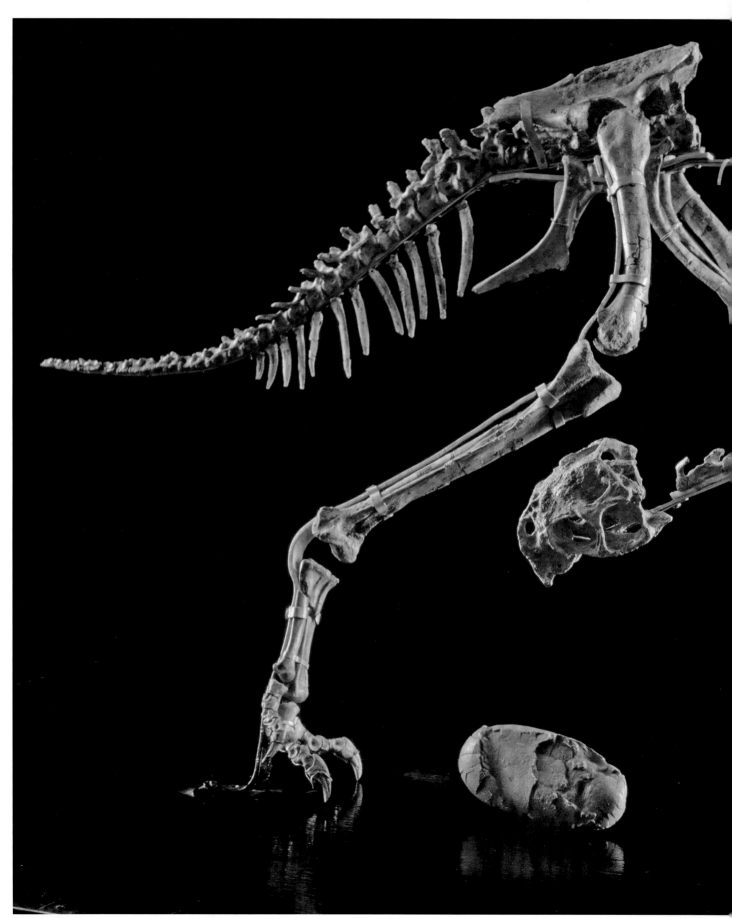

• ORDER • Saurischia **• FAMILY •** Oviraptoridae **• GENUS & SPECIES •** *Oviraptor philoceratops, O. mongoliensis*

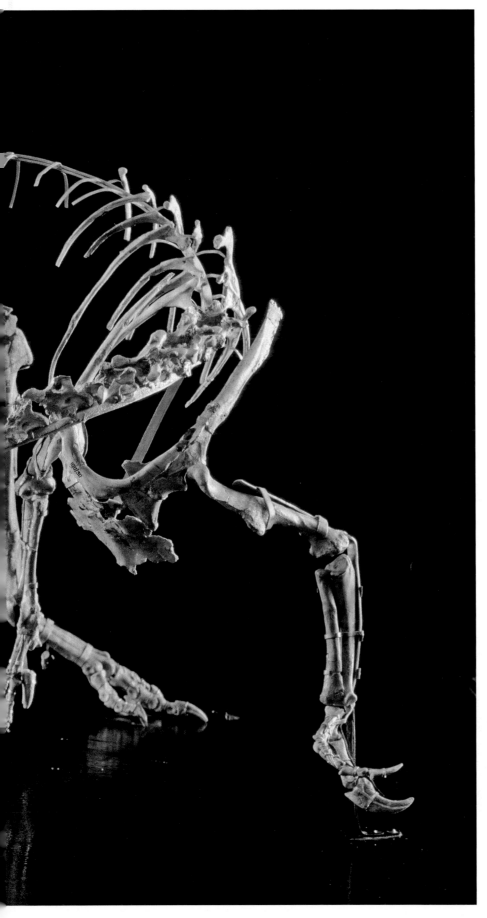

A GIANT OVIRAPTORID IN CHINA

In 2005, the fossil of a giant birdlike dinosaur thought to belong to the oviraptorid group was found in China. News of the find did not break until 2007. The location was the Erlian Basin in the Chinese region of Inner Mongolia, where the giant was discovered by accident. A team from the Institute of Vertebrate Paleontology and Paleoanthropology in Beijing, headed by the famous Chinese fossil finder Xu Xing, was showing reporters how previous fossils had been found when they happened upon the 3 ft (1 m)-long leg bone of a young adult. On examination, the giant dinosaur was found to be as large as some tyrannosaurs, which made it more than six times taller than the "standard" oviraptorid. The find, named the *Gigantoraptor*, was estimated to be 26 ft (8 m) long, 16 ft (5 m) tall and to weigh 1.38 tons (1,400 kg). Although some paleontologists were surprised that an oviraptorid could be so enormous, Philip Currie of the University of Alberta, in Canada, has suggested that animals tended to become larger as evolution went on because their size made it easier for them to find food, attract mates, and fight off predators.

Troodon

VITAL STATISTICS

FOSSIL LOCATION	North America
DIET	Carnivorous
PRONUNCIATION	TROH-don
WEIGHT	130 lb (60 kg)
LENGTH	6 ft 6 in (2 m)
HEIGHT	39 in (1 m)
MEANING OF NAME	"Wounding tooth"

FOSSIL EVIDENCE

Troodon fossils were discovered in North America in places hundreds of miles apart from each other and separated by up to 10 million years. This makes it very unlikely that they belonged to a single species of *Troodon*, but it remains unknown how many species there were. A *Troodon* tooth was the first fossil found (in 1901,) followed in 1932 by a foot, a hand, and vertebrae. A special feature of the foot was the enlarged claw attached to the second toe.

DINOSAUR

LATE CRETACEOUS

Troodon, one of the first dinosaurs to be found in North America, was discovered in 1855. It was quite small and lived around 75 million years ago in what is now the United States and Canada. Based on its long, narrow limbs, it was probably a quick mover. Some paleontologists believe it was an omnivore that ate plants but also hunted insects and other creatures smaller than itself, such as lizards. *Troodon* has been classed as one of the most intelligent non-avian dinosaurs because it had a large brain compared to the size of its body.

HEAD
Troodon was a bird-like dinosaur with a head that probably looked like the head of the present-day ostrich.

CLAWS
Troodon may have been quite small, but the large, curved claws on its hands and feet made it a very dangerous predator.

• **ORDER** • Saurischia • **FAMILY** • Troodontidae • **GENUS & SPECIES** • *Troodon formosus*

WHERE IN THE WORLD?

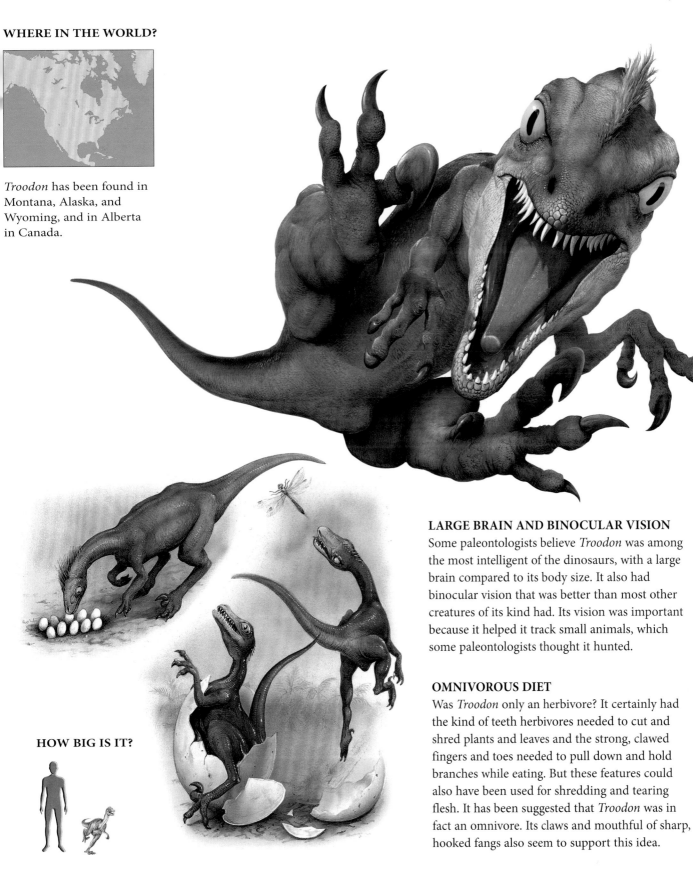

Troodon has been found in Montana, Alaska, and Wyoming, and in Alberta in Canada.

HOW BIG IS IT?

LARGE BRAIN AND BINOCULAR VISION

Some paleontologists believe *Troodon* was among the most intelligent of the dinosaurs, with a large brain compared to its body size. It also had binocular vision that was better than most other creatures of its kind had. Its vision was important because it helped it track small animals, which some paleontologists thought it hunted.

OMNIVOROUS DIET

Was *Troodon* only an herbivore? It certainly had the kind of teeth herbivores needed to cut and shred plants and leaves and the strong, clawed fingers and toes needed to pull down and hold branches while eating. But these features could also have been used for shredding and tearing flesh. It has been suggested that *Troodon* was in fact an omnivore. Its claws and mouthful of sharp, hooked fangs also seem to support this idea.

TIMELINE (millions of years ago)

10	505	438	408	360	280	248	208	146	65	1.8 to today

Velociraptor

VITAL STATISTICS

Fossil Location	Mongolia, Chinese Inner Mongolia
Diet	Carnivorous
Pronunciation	Vel-ossi-RAP-tor
Weight	33 lb (15 kg)
Length	7 ft (2 m)
Height	1 ft 7 in (0.5 m) at the hip
Meaning of name	"Swift thief"

FOSSIL EVIDENCE

Around 12 fossil skeletons of *Velociraptor* have been discovered, more than any other member of the birdlike dromaeosaurid family. *Velociraptor*'s teeth were made for slicing meat, with up to 28 of them spaced along each side of its jaw. The teeth were serrated front and back, a feature that helped *Velociraptor* slice the flesh of its prey. *Velociraptor*'s hands with their three strong claws were built in the same way as the wing bones of modern birds.

DINOSAUR

LATE CRETACEOUS

Velociraptor had feathers, a long tail, and claws on all its fingers and toes. The claws were probably used to kill *Velociraptor*'s prey. It appears to have lived in a dry environment full of sand dunes but very little water. *Protoceratops* might have been on the menu for *Velociraptor*. In 1971, a find that came to be known as the Fighting Dinosaurs was discovered. In this find, *Protoceratops* and *Velociraptor* were found locked together in deadly combat.

WHERE IN THE WORLD?

Velociraptor was found at Omnogovi and Tugrugeen Shireh in Mongolia and in Chinese Inner Mongolia.

CLAWS
Sickle-shaped claws on its feet measured more than 2.5 in (6.5 cm) each.

HOW BIG IS IT?

• **ORDER** • Saurischia • **FAMILY** • Dromaeosauridae • **GENUS & SPECIES** • *Velociraptor mongoliensis, V. osmolskae*

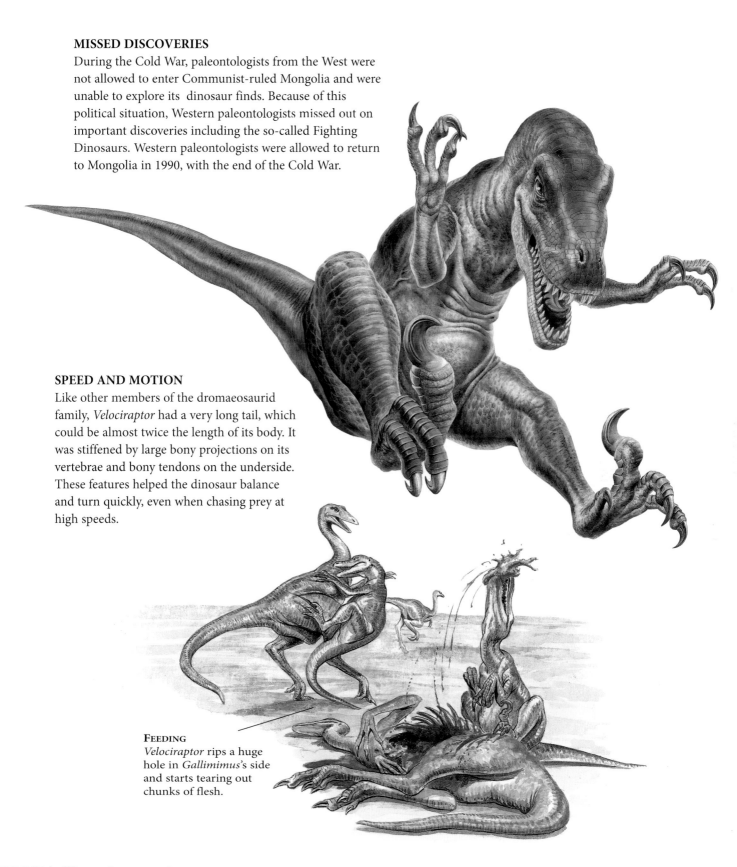

MISSED DISCOVERIES

During the Cold War, paleontologists from the West were not allowed to enter Communist-ruled Mongolia and were unable to explore its dinosaur finds. Because of this political situation, Western paleontologists missed out on important discoveries including the so-called Fighting Dinosaurs. Western paleontologists were allowed to return to Mongolia in 1990, with the end of the Cold War.

SPEED AND MOTION

Like other members of the dromaeosaurid family, *Velociraptor* had a very long tail, which could be almost twice the length of its body. It was stiffened by large bony projections on its vertebrae and bony tendons on the underside. These features helped the dinosaur balance and turn quickly, even when chasing prey at high speeds.

FEEDING
Velociraptor rips a huge hole in *Gallimimus*'s side and starts tearing out chunks of flesh.

IMELINE (millions of years ago)

| 40 | 505 | 438 | 408 | 360 | 280 | 248 | 208 | 146 | 65 | 1.8 to today |

Velociraptor

• **ORDER** • Saurischia • **FAMILY** • Dromaeosauridae • **GENUS & SPECIES** • *Velociraptor mongoliensis, V. osmolskae*

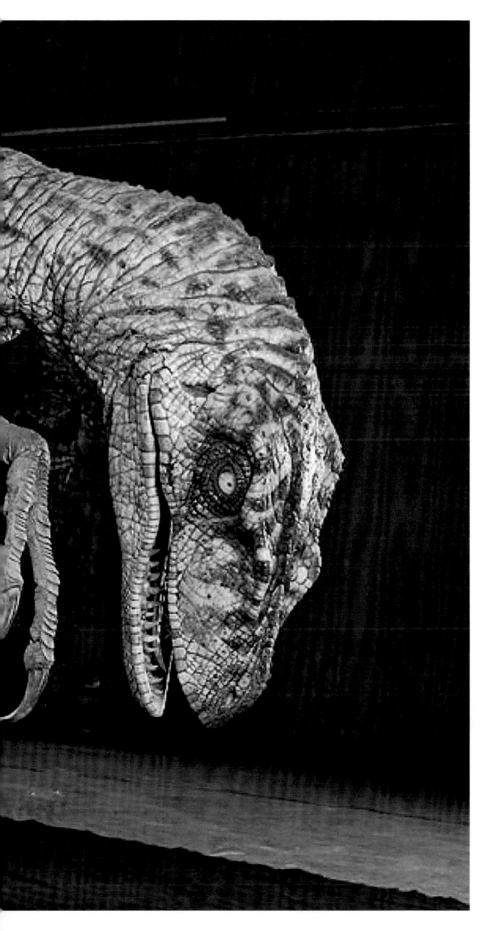

EVIDENCE OF FEATHERS

Velociraptor was first discovered in Mongolia in 1922, long before birds were definitely recognized as dinosaurs. When this idea began to take hold in the 1960s, scientists began to think that *Velociraptor*, since was it was so close to birds, was feathered. But they didn't think it could fly. In September 2007, a fossil find proved that Velociraptor did indeed have feathers. A study made on the bones of a *Velociraptor* forearm found in Mongolia showed rows of small bumps. Scientists figured out that these were quill knobs or anchors for feathers. Based on this, scientists felt confident that *Velociraptor* had feathers. When this discovery was added to the many other similarities between *Velociraptor* and modern birds, it became even clearer that in spite of the millions of years between them, birds and *Velociraptors* had a lot in common. As Mark Norell, curator in charge of fossil reptiles, amphibians, and birds at the American Museum of Natural History, put it, "The more we learn about these animals, the more we find that there is basically no difference between birds and their closely related dinosaur ancestors like *Velociraptor*. Both have wishbones, brooded their nests, possessed hollow bones, and were covered in feathers. If animals like *Velociraptor* were still alive today, our first impression would be that they were just very unusual-looking birds."

Mononykus

• ORDER • Saurischia • FAMILY • Alvarezsauridae • GENUS & SPECIES • *Mononykus olecran*

VITAL STATISTICS

FOSSIL LOCATION	Mongolia
DIET	Carnivorous, possibly omnivorous
PRONUNCIATION	MON-o-NYE-kus
WEIGHT	Unknown
LENGTH	3 ft (90 cm)
HEIGHT	Unknown
MEANING OF NAME	"Single claw" because of the unusual digits on its forelimbs

FOSSIL EVIDENCE

Light, hollow bones do not fossilize well, so the remains of *Mononykus* are incomplete. The most interesting feature is the large single claw at the end of each short, muscular arm. It was not likely used for snatching prey or for digging and has led some paleontologists to suggest *Mononykus* used it to break open termite mounds in search of food. Its large eyes may have allowed *Mononykus* to hunt at night, and it may have eaten plant food as well as insects and lizards.

DINOSAUR

LATE CRETACEOUS

Is it a bird? Is it a birdlike dinosaur? Early opinion was divided because *Mononykus* is so closely related to birds. This was a small, fast, sharp-eyed predator that roamed open desert plains.

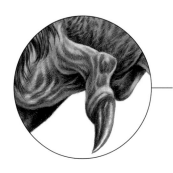

STERNUM AND FIBULA
The small, keeled sternum and fibula have led some scientists to suggest *Mononykus* was an early bird and not a non-avian dinosaur.

WHERE IN THE WORLD?

Remains have been found in the Bugin Tsav region of the Gobi Desert in southeastern Mongolia.

LEGS
Long, strong legs would have helped *Mononykus* make a speedy escape if it met a dangerous predator.

HOW BIG IS IT?

TIMELINE (millions of years ago)

540	505	438	408	360	280	248	208	146	65	1.8 to today

Glossary

biodiversity (by-oh-dih-VER-si-tee) When an environment contains many different types of plants and animals

camouflage (KAM-uh-flawj) To disguise by blending in with the surroundings

cannibalism (KAN-ih-bul-izm) When one animal eats another animal of the same kind, such as a human eating another human

digits (DIH-jits) Divisions of a limb, such as a fingers

fenestrae (feh-NES-tree) Hollow openings in the bone

flash flood (flash FLUD) A sudden flood of water that occurs very quickly and is usually caused by heavy rain

fossil (FAH-sil) Remains or traces of an organism from the past that have been preserved, such as bones, teeth, footprints, etc.

gracile (GRAH-sul) Small and slender

omnivore (AHM-nih-vor) Something that eats both plants and meat

paleontologist (pay-lee-on-TAH-luh-jist) A scientist who studies fossils

scavenger (SKAH-ven-jer) Animals that usually do not kill their own food, but feed on the carcasses left behind by other predators

serrated (seh-RAY-ted) Notched or toothed on the edge

sickle (SIH-kul) A tool with a half-moon shaped curved blade and a short handle

Index

For More Information

Books

Dingus, Lowell, Rodolfo Coria, and Luis M. Chiappe. *Dinosaur Eggs Discovered!: Unscrambling the Clues.* Minneapolis, MN: Twenty-First Century Books, 2008.

Gray, Susan Heinrichs. *Velociraptor.* Mankato, MN: Child's World, 2004.

Holmes, Thom. *Feathered Dinosaurs: The Origin of Birds.* Berkeley Heights, NJ: Enslow Publishers, 2002.

Web Sites

To ensure the currency and safety of recommended Internet links, Windmill maintains and updates an online list of sites related to the subject of this book. To access this list of Web sites, please go to www.windmillbooks.com/weblinks and select this book's title.

For more great fiction and nonfiction,
go to www.windmillbooks.com.